Pebble® Plus

All about Spring

People in Spring

by Martha E. H. Rustad

Consulting Editor: Gail Saunders-Smith, PhD

Consultant: John D. Krenz, PhD
Department of Biological Sciences
Minnesota State University, Mankato

T0050987

CAPSTONE PRESS
a capstone imprint

Pebble Plus is published by Capstone Press,
1710 Roe Crest Drive, North Mankato, Minnesota 56003.
www.capstonepub.com

Copyright © 2013 by Capstone Press, a Capstone imprint. All rights reserved.
No part of this publication may be reproduced in whole or in part, or stored in a retrieval system, or transmitted in any form or by any means, electronic, mechanical, photocopying, recording, or otherwise, without written permission of the publisher. For information regarding permission, write to Capstone Press,
1710 Roe Crest Drive, North Mankato, Minnesota 56003.

Library of Congress Cataloging-in-Publication Data
Rustad, Martha E. H. (Martha Elizabeth Hillman), 1975-
People in spring / by Martha E.H. Rustad.
p. cm. — (Pebble plus. All about spring)
ISBN 978-1-4296-8657-0 (library binding)
ISBN 978-1-4296-9361-5 (paperback)
ISBN 978-1-62065-287-9 (ebook PDF)
1. Human beings—Effect of climate on—Juvenile literature. 2. Spring—Juvenile literature. I. Title.
Includes bibliographical references and index.
GF71.R87 2013

508.2—dc23
2012000293
Summary: "Simple text and full-color photographs present people in spring."

Editorial Credits
Shelly Lyons, editor; Bobbie Nuytten, designer; Svetlana Zhurkin, photo researcher; Kathy McColley, production specialist

Photo Credits
Alamy: Henry George Beeker, 4–5; Capstone Studio: Karon Dubke, 12–13; Dreamstime: Monkey Business Images, 10–11, 18–19; Getty Images: Lori Adamski Peek, 16–17; iStockphoto: Joshua Hodge Photography, 8–9, Todd Keith, 20–21, Yenwen Lu, 14–15; Shutterstock: Alena Ozerova, cover, 6–7, Marish (green leaf), cover and throughout, mypokcik, 1, Zubada (leaf pattern), cover

Note to Parents and Teachers

The All about Spring series supports national science and social studies standards related to changes during the seasons. This book describes and illustrates people in spring. The images support early readers in understanding the text. The repetition of words and phrases helps early readers learn new words. This book also introduces early readers to subject-specific vocabulary words, which are defined in the Glossary section. Early readers may need assistance to read some words and to use the Table of Contents, Glossary, Read More, Internet Sites, and Index sections of the book.

Printed in the United States 4353

Table of Contents

Spring Is Here 4
What We Do 6
Looking Forward 12
Spring Celebrations 16

Glossary 22
Read More 23
Internet Sites. 23
Index 24

Spring Is Here

It's spring.

The days are getting longer.

Warmer weather is here.

What We Do

We wear light jackets outdoors.

An umbrella keeps us dry.

The last weeks of school
are in spring.
Soon summer break
will be here.

We go on nature walks.

We hear young birds chirp.

Looking Forward

In spring, we plant seeds.
We wait for green sprouts
to grow.

We watch for

blooming buds.

Spring flowers smell sweet.

Spring Celebrations

On April 22, we celebrate

Earth Day.

We learn how to protect nature.

In May, we honor moms
on Mother's Day.
We thank dads in June
on Father's Day.

In spring, we see young animals
and new plants.
What else do you see
in spring?

Glossary

bud—a small shoot on a plant that grows into a leaf or flower

celebrate—to do something fun on a special day

honor—to give praise or show respect

nature—everything in the world that isn't made by people

seed—part of a flower that will grow into a new plant

sprout—a young plant that has just appeared above the ground

Read More

Bullard, Lisa. *Earth Day Every Day.* Planet Protectors. Minneapolis: Millbrook Press, 2012.

Pfeffer, Wendy. *A New Beginning: Celebrating the Spring Equinox.* New York: Dutton Children's Books, 2008.

Smith, Siân. *Changing Seasons.* Chicago: Heinemann Library, 2009.

Internet Sites

FactHound offers a safe, fun way to find Internet sites related to this book. All of the sites on FactHound have been researched by our staff.

Here's all you do:

Visit *www.facthound.com*

Type in this code: 9781429686570

Index

animals, 20
birds, 10
Earth Day, 16
Father's Day, 18
flowers, 14
jackets, 6
longer days, 4
Mother's Day, 18
nature walks, 10
plants, 12, 14, 20
school, 8
seeds, 12
sprouts, 12
umbrellas, 6
weather, 4

Word Count: 110
Grade: 1
Early-Intervention Level: 13